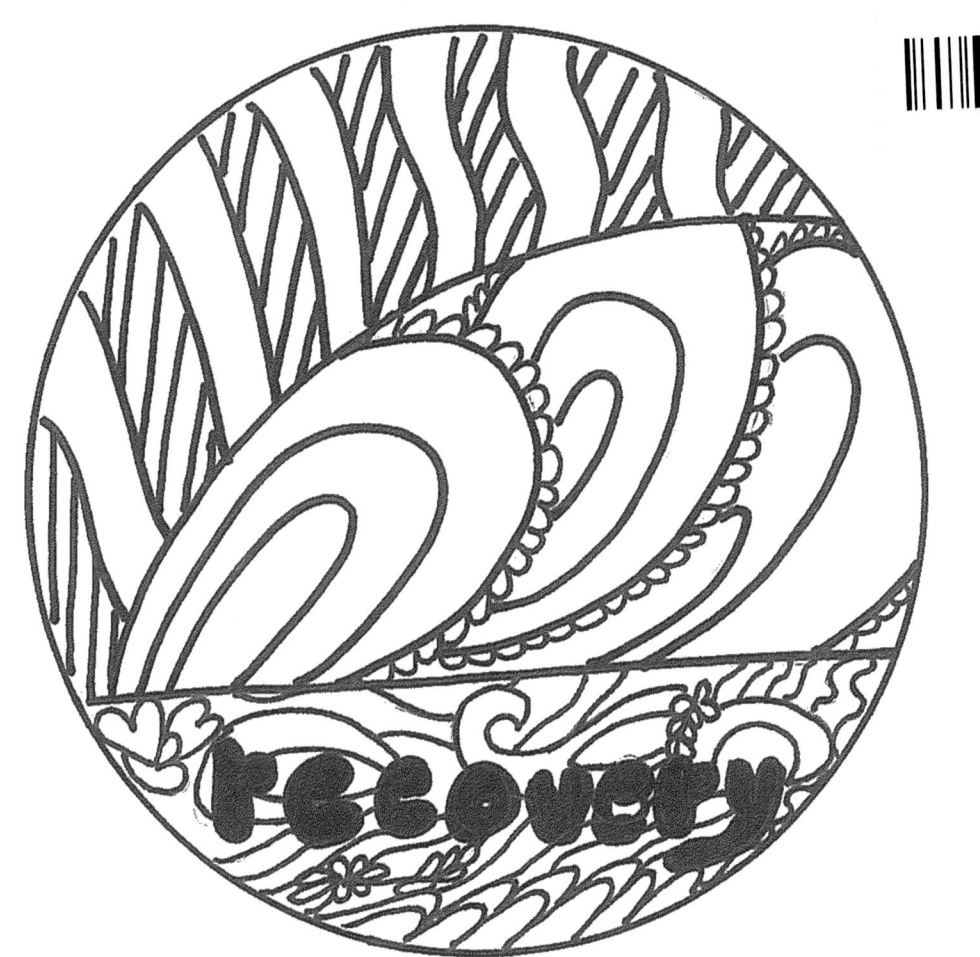

Coloring for Recovery from Binge Eating Disorder: Original Art and Journaling Prompts

by Christina Fisanick Greer, Ph.D.,
   The Optimistic Addict

Rhetorica Media
142 Edgington Lane
Wheeling, WV 26003
www.optimisticfoodaddict.com

How to Use this Book

Welcome to *Coloring for Recovery*! This book was born out of my twin loves: coloring and writing. In it, you will find beautiful, hand drawn black and white images ready to color. While you are coloring each image, meditate on the quote below it. Then, when you are finished, spend some time responding to the reflection questions posted on the opposite page.

Every part of this book is designed to get you thinking critically about recovery from binge eating disorder. Studies show that coloring is a great way to relieve stress and that writing about recovery is a powerful healing tool.

For more resources, please see my website at www.optimisticfoodaddict.com or my Facebook page at https://www.facebook.com/theoptimisticfoodaddict/.

A Word About the Author/Artist

I have been teaching writing on the university level for 20 years and am the author of more than 30 books.

I entered recovery from binge eating disorder after suffering for close to 30 years. Soon after, I founded a support group for suffers of food addiction on Facebook, which now has nearly 7,000 members.

My next book, *The Optimistic Addict: Recovering from Binge Eating Disorder*, will be published by MSI Press in late summer 2016.

I hope this book helps you on your journey! Please share your final colored images and your words with me. I love to see how others transform my work and make it their own. You can find me at the above locations or through email at clfisanick@aol.com.

Christina Fisanick Greer, Ph.D.
The Optimistic Addict

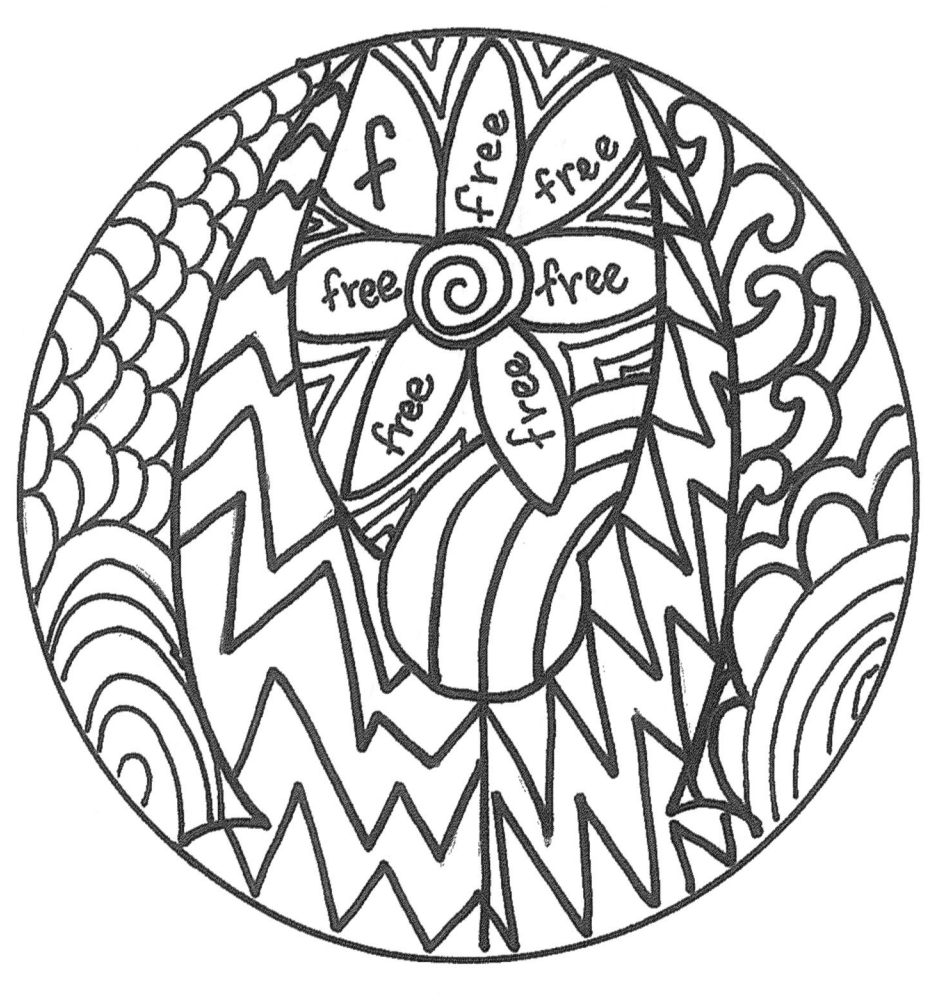

"From food addiction to food serenity — freedom tastes great!"

~Vera Tarman, Food Junkies: The Truth about Food Addiction

What does freedom mean to you in the context of binge eating and your relationship with food? How does it feel to be free of the bondage of compulsive eating?

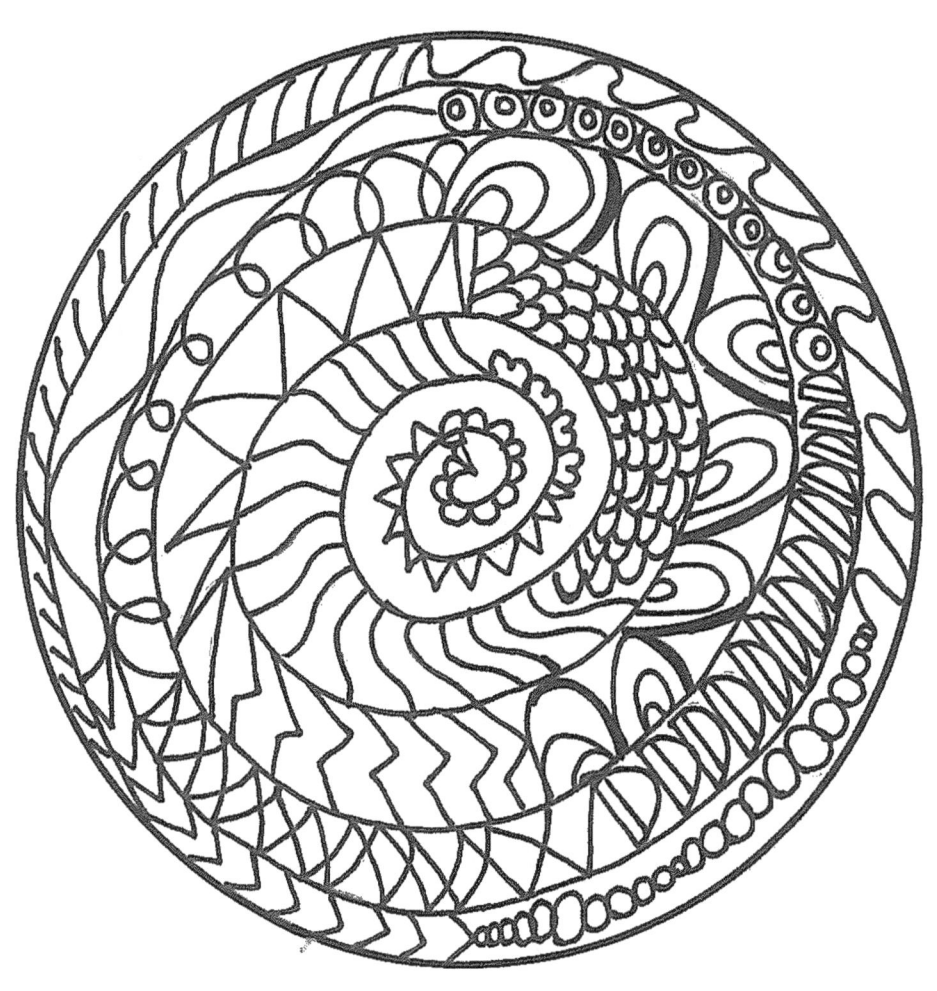

"My binge eating was just a cover-up for the larger issue: Trying to fill the emptiness." ~SARK, Transformation Soup: Healing for the Splendidly Imperfect

Read > Reflect > Write

What are you eating to cover up? What are you trying to hide in the food?

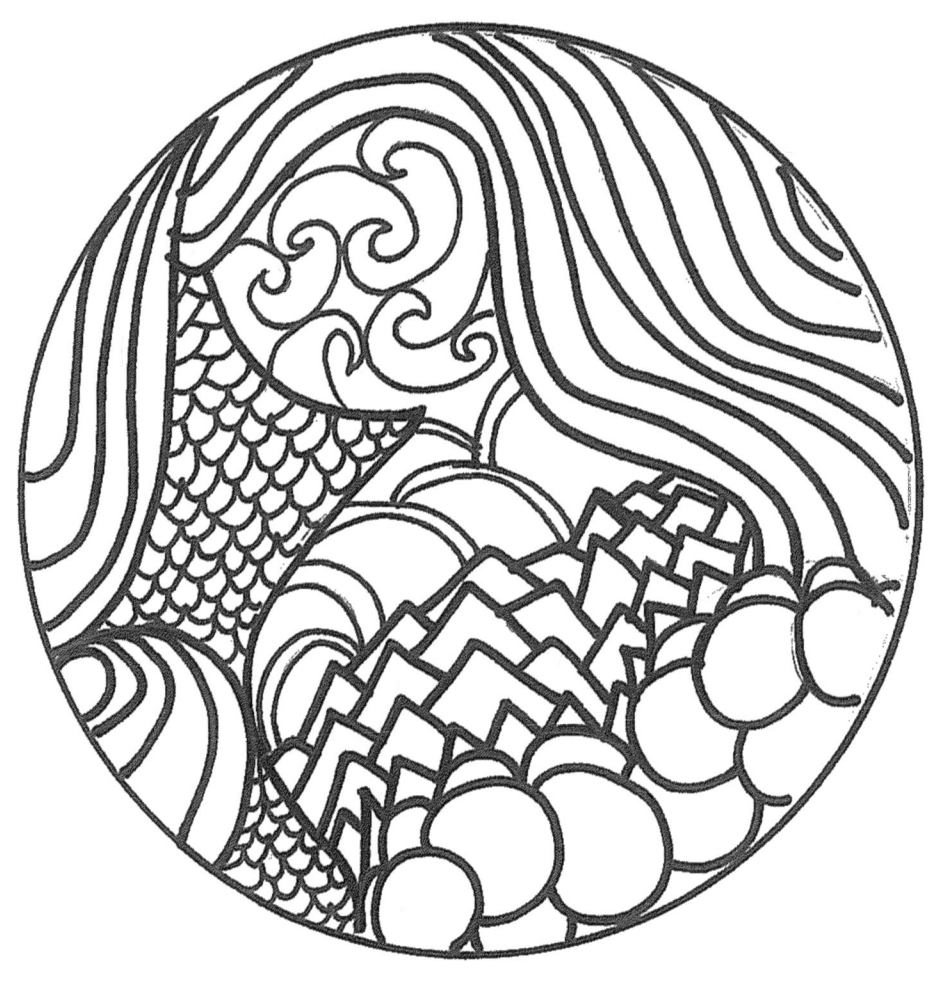

"A cultural fixation on female thinness is not an obsession about female beauty but an obsession about female obedience."

~Naomi Wolf, The Beauty Myth

Read > Reflect > Write

Have you been obsessed with being thin? What role has dieting played in the development of your food addiction? Do you agree that dieting isn't about beauty but about control and obedience?

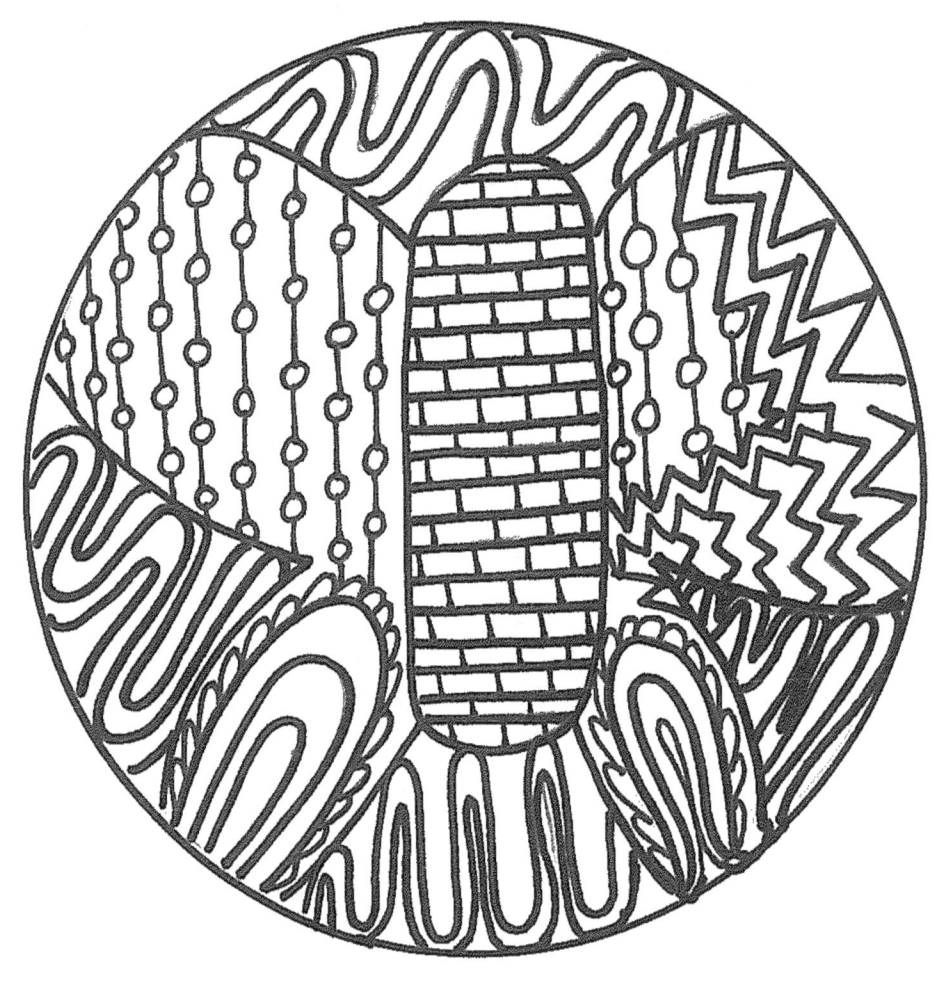

"Eating disorders are prevalent among women who were sexually abused as children. They seem to have components of other symptoms such as obsessions, compulsions, avoidance of food, and anxiety, and they primarily include a distorted body image and feelings of body shame." —Karen A. Duncan, Healing from the Trauma of Childhood Sexual Abuse: The Journey for Women

Read > Reflect > Write

Were you sexual abused as a child? Do you think your eating disorder is a result of that abuse? What purpose does binge eating serve you in this regard?

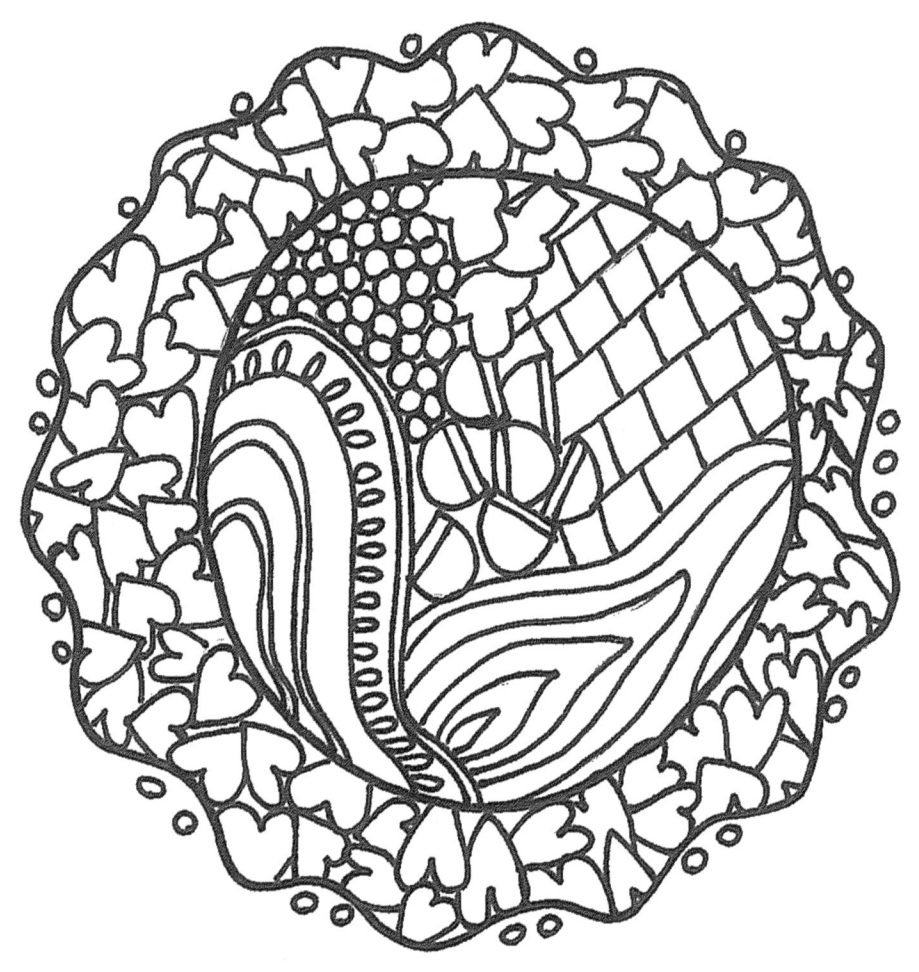

"We clean our plates, yet we're still famished—starving for
something other than food."   ~Kate Wicker, Weight Less

Read > Reflect > Write

What are you starving for? Love? Acceptance? What?

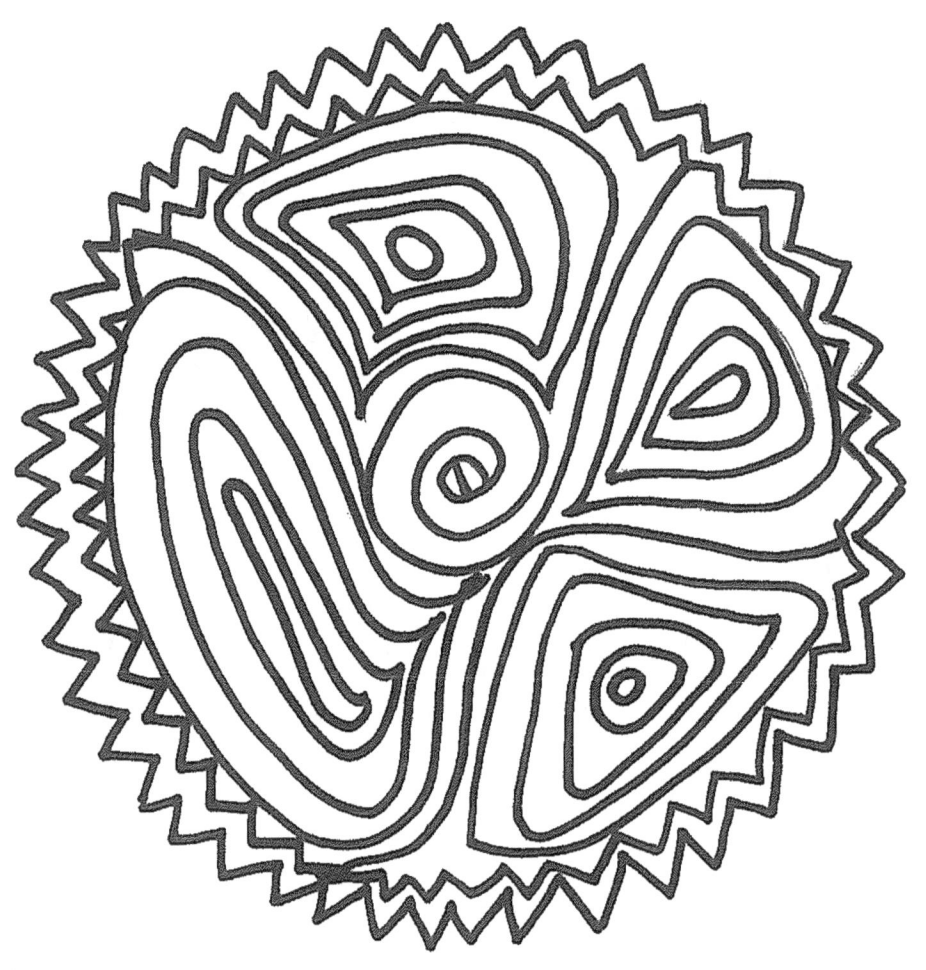

"And, what' s more, this 'precious' body, the very same that is hooted and honked at, demeaned both in daily life as well as in ever existing form of media, harrassed, molested, raped, and, if all that wasn' t enough, is forever poked and prodded and weighed and constantly wrong for eating too much, eating too little, a million details which all point to the solitary girl, to EVERY solitary girl, and say: Destroy yourself." ~Emilie Autumn,

Read > Reflect > Write

How is your eating disorder destroying YOU? How are YOU destroying
YOU?

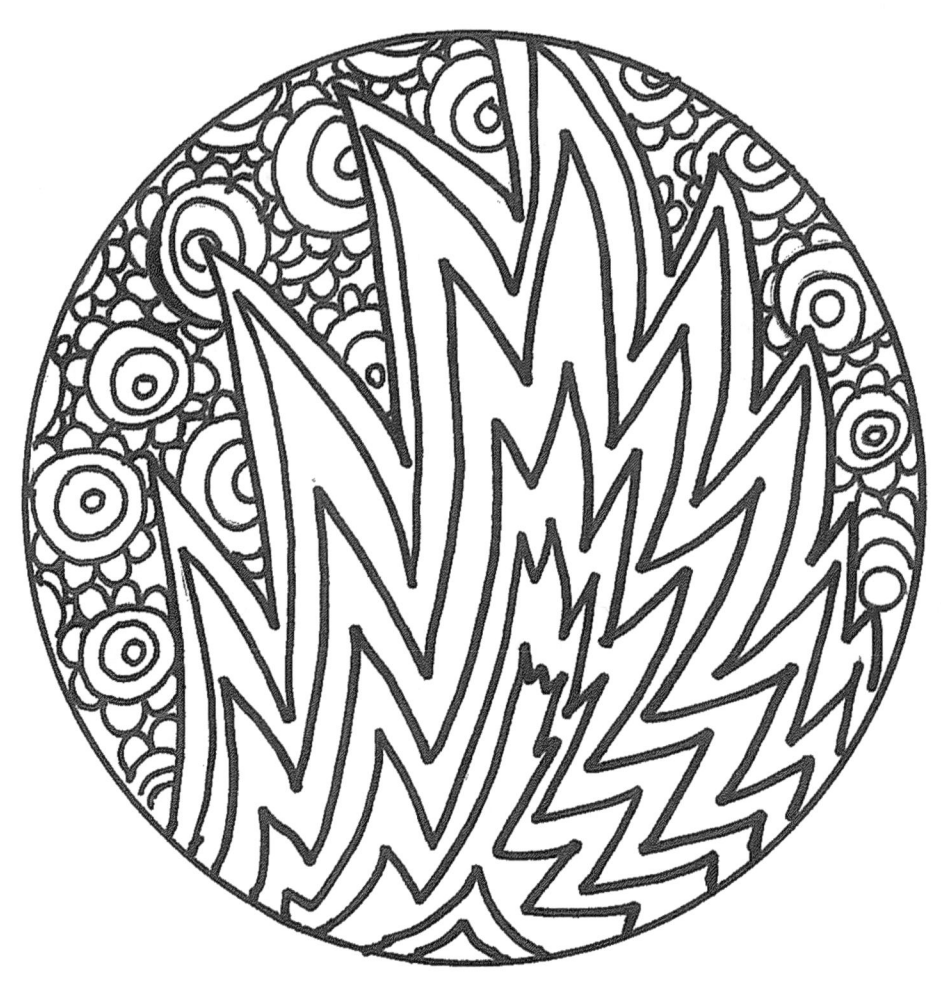

"I wish I had cancer. I will burn in hell for that, but it's true." ~Laurie Halse Anderson, Wintergirls

Read > Reflect > Write

How many times have you wished that you had a disease that would make you thin? Or any disease other than an eating disorder?

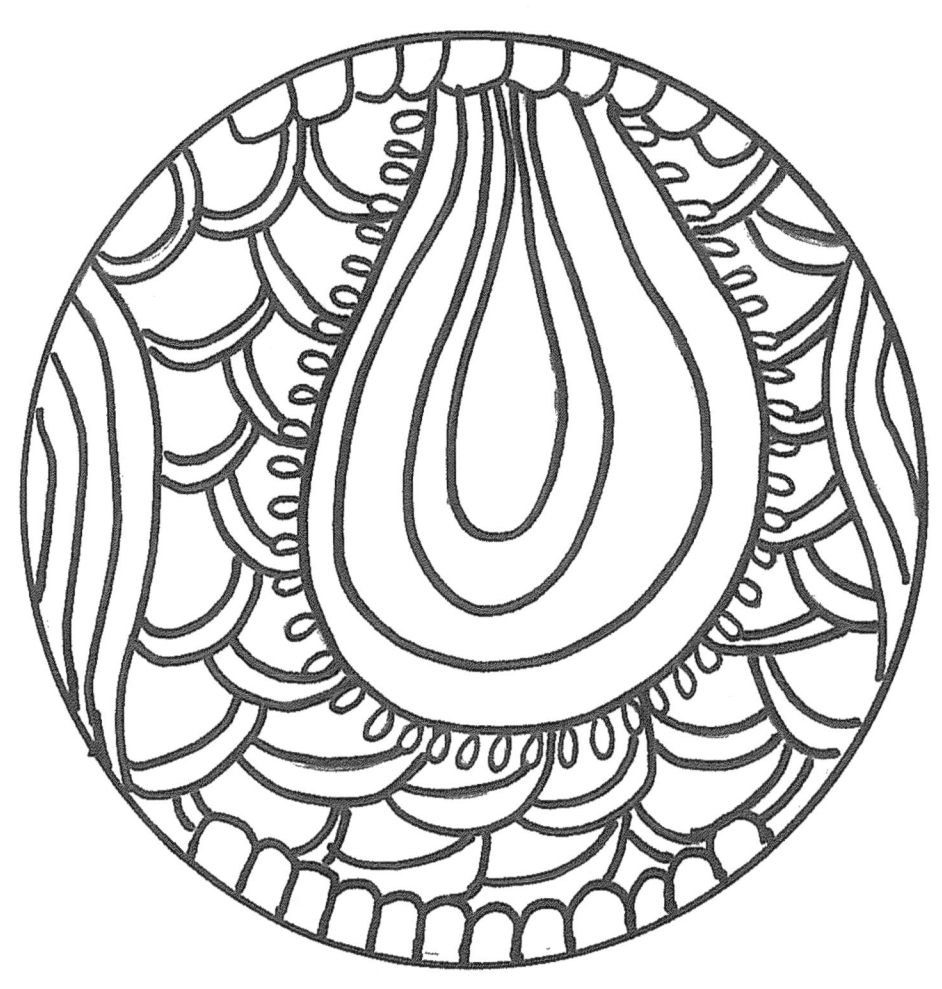

"I am forever engaged in a silent battle in my head over whether or not to lift the fork to my mouth, and when I talk myself into doing so, I taste only shame." ~Jena Morrow, Hollow

Read > Reflect > Write

Shame is a powerful part of the binge eating cycle. What role does shame play in the way you live with food addiction? Are there ways to overcome that shame?

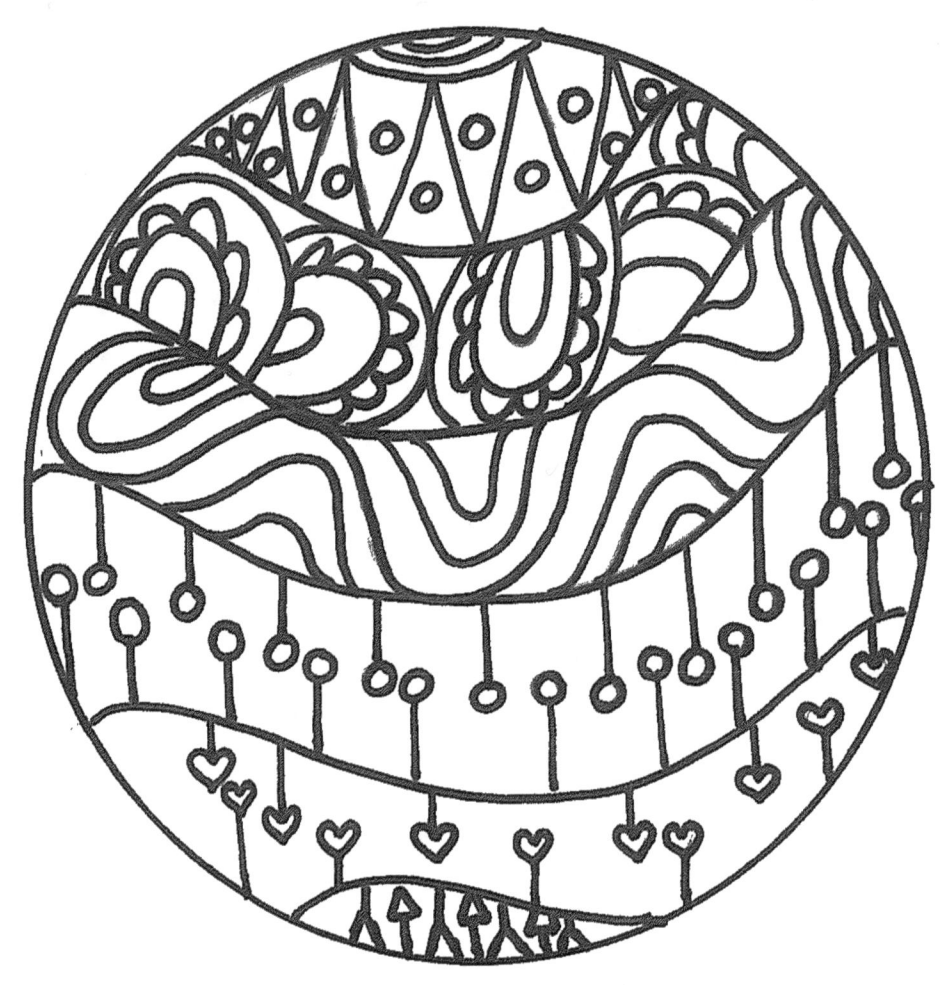

"I am beginning to measure myself in strength, not pounds. Sometimes in smiles." ~Laurie Halse Anderson, Wintergirls

Read > Reflect > Write

How do you measure yourself? What is a good day for you now that you are not focused on the scale? How do you define success in life beyond weight and pants size?

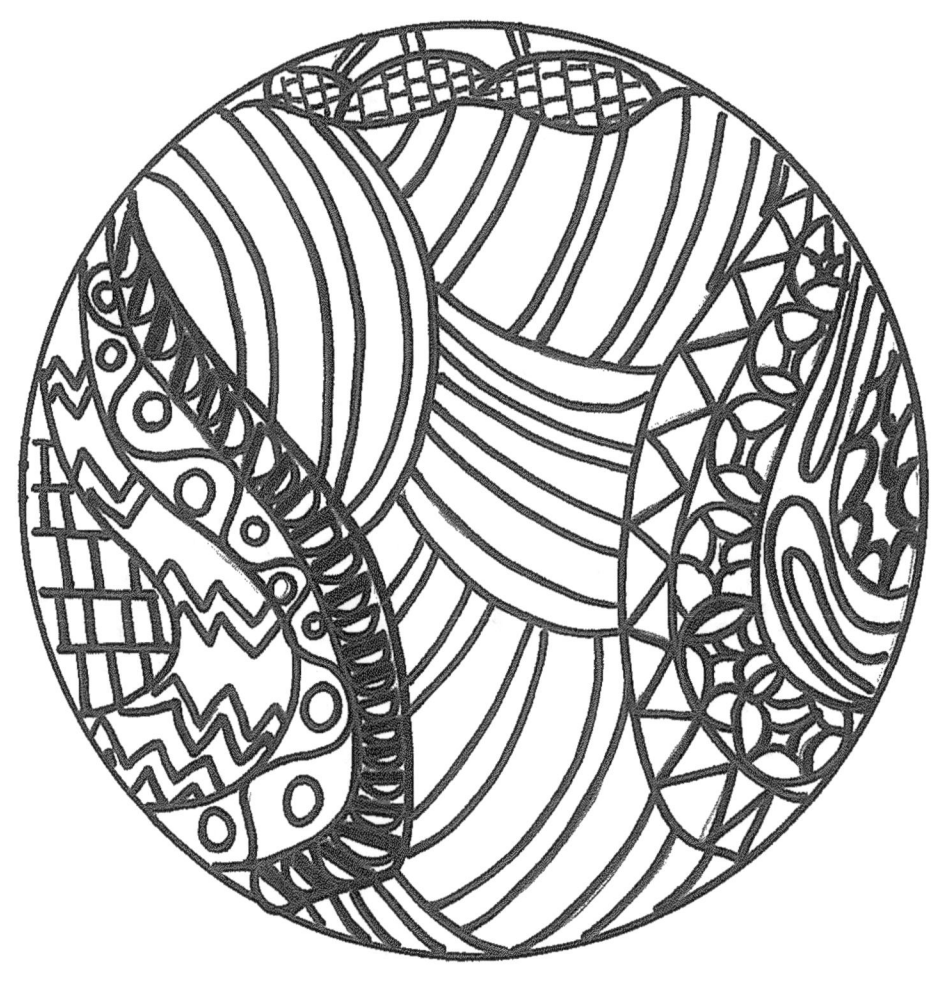

"We don't want to EAT hot fudge sundaes as much as we want our lives to BE hot fudge sundaes. We want to come home to ourselves."
~Geneen Roth, Women, Food and God

Read > Reflect > Write

What does Roth mean by this statement? How can we BE hot fudge sundaes? How can we come home to ourselves? How can you come home to yourself?

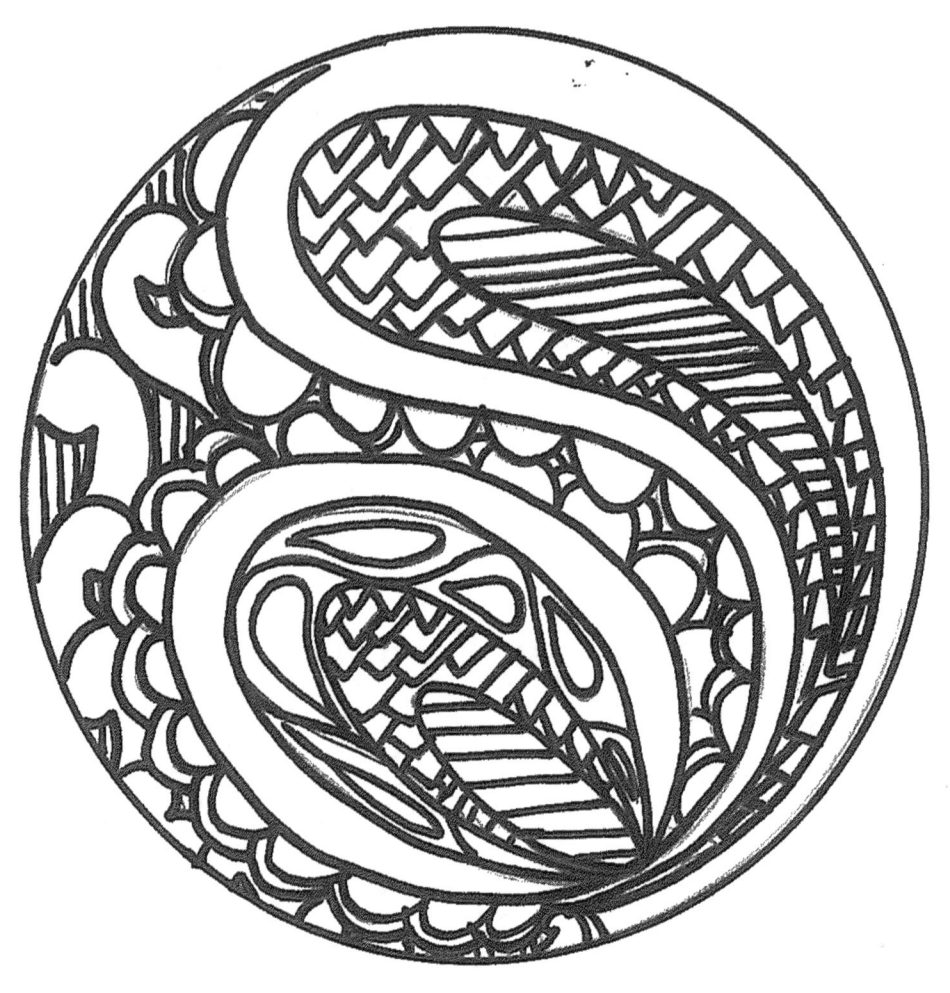

"Denial — a major symptom of food and other addictions — is a psychological mechanism humans use to protect themselves from fear by blocking conscious awareness of truth. Denial by food addicts consists of blocking awareness of excessive and inappropriate use of food and resulting harmful consequences." Kay Sheppard, author of Food Addiction: Your Body Knows

Read > Reflect > Write

Are you in denial about how much you eat? Where you eat? The consequences of your compulsive eating? What are some steps you can take to overcome that denial and be honest with yourself?

www.ingramcontent.com/pod-product-compliance
Lightning Source LLC
Chambersburg PA
CBHW080359290526
45791CB00009BA/2931